# TRANZLATY

## Language is for everyone
言語はすべての人のためのもの

# Beauty and the Beast

# 美女と野獣

Gabrielle-Suzanne Barbot
de Villeneuve

English / 日本語

Copyright © 2025 Tranzlaty
All rights reserved
Published by Tranzlaty
ISBN: 978-1-83566-978-5
Original text by Gabrielle-Suzanne Barbot de Villeneuve
La Belle et la Bête
First published in French in 1740
Taken from The Blue Fairy Book (Andrew Lang)
Illustration by Walter Crane
www.tranzlaty.com

There was once a rich merchant
昔、裕福な商人がいました
this rich merchant had six children
この裕福な商人には6人の子供がいた
he had three sons and three daughters
彼には3人の息子と3人の娘がいた
he spared no cost for their education
彼は子供たちの教育に惜しみない費用をかけた
because he was a man of sense
彼は賢明な人だったから
but he gave his children many servants
しかし彼は子供たちに多くの召使いを与えた
his daughters were extremely pretty
彼の娘たちはとても可愛かった
and his youngest daughter was especially pretty
そして彼の末娘は特に可愛かった
as a child her Beauty was already admired
子供の頃から彼女の美しさは賞賛されていた
and the people called her by her Beauty
人々は彼女の美しさから彼女を呼んだ
her Beauty did not fade as she got older
彼女の美しさは年を重ねても衰えなかった
so the people kept calling her by her Beauty
人々は彼女の美しさから彼女を呼び続けた
this made her sisters very jealous
これには姉妹たちも嫉妬した
the two eldest daughters had a great deal of pride
二人の長女は大きな誇りを持っていた
their wealth was the source of their pride
彼らの富は彼らの誇りの源であった
and they didn't hide their pride either
そして彼らはプライドも隠さなかった
they did not visit other merchants' daughters
彼らは他の商人の娘を訪ねることはなかった
because they only meet with aristocracy

彼らは貴族としか会わないから
they went out every day to parties
彼らは毎日パーティーに出かけた
balls, plays, concerts, and so forth
舞踏会、演劇、コンサートなど
and they laughed at their youngest sister
そして彼らは末の妹を笑った
because she spent most of her time reading
彼女はほとんどの時間を読書に費やしていたので
it was well known that they were wealthy
彼らが裕福であることはよく知られていた
so several eminent merchants asked for their hand
そこで何人かの著名な商人が彼らに協力を求めた
but they said they were not going to marry
しかし彼らは結婚するつもりはないと言った
but they were prepared to make some exceptions
しかし、彼らはいくつかの例外を認める用意があった
"perhaps I could marry a Duke"
「公爵と結婚できるかもしれない」
"I guess I could marry an Earl"
「伯爵と結婚できるかもしれない」
Beauty very civilly thanked those that proposed to her
美女はプロポーズしてくれた人たちにとても丁寧に感謝した
she told them she was still too young to marry
彼女は結婚するにはまだ若すぎると言った
she wanted to stay a few more years with her father
彼女は父親とあと数年一緒にいたかった
All at once the merchant lost his fortune
突然、商人は財産を失った
he lost everything apart from a small country house
彼は小さな田舎の家以外すべてを失った
and he told his children with tears in his eyes:
そして彼は目に涙を浮かべながら子供たちにこう言いました。

"we must go to the countryside"
「田舎に行かなくてはならない」
"and we must work for our living"
「そして私たちは生活のために働かなければなりません」
the two eldest daughters didn't want to leave the town
二人の長女は町を離れたくなかった
they had several lovers in the city
彼らには市内に数人の愛人がいた
and they were sure one of their lovers would marry them
そして彼らは恋人の一人が結婚してくれると確信していた
they thought their lovers would marry them even with no fortune
彼らは財産がなくても恋人が結婚してくれると信じていた
but the good ladies were mistaken
しかし、その善良な女性たちは間違っていた
their lovers abandoned them very quickly
彼らの恋人たちはすぐに彼らを捨てた
because they had no fortunes any more
彼らにはもう財産がなかったから
this showed they were not actually well liked
これは彼らが実際にはあまり好かれていなかったことを示している
everybody said they do not deserve to be pitied
誰もが同情されるに値しないと言った
"we are glad to see their pride humbled"
「彼らのプライドが謙虚になったことを嬉しく思います」
"let them be proud of milking cows"
「牛の乳搾りを誇りに思ってもらいましょう」
but they were concerned for Beauty
しかし彼らは美を気にしていた
she was such a sweet creature

彼女は本当に優しい人でした
she spoke so kindly to poor people
彼女は貧しい人々にとても優しく話しかけた
and she was of such an innocent nature
彼女はとても純粋な性格だった
Several gentlemen would have married her
何人かの紳士が彼女と結婚しただろう
they would have married her even though she was poor
彼女は貧しかったが、彼らは彼女と結婚しただろう
but she told them she couldn't marry them
しかし彼女は結婚できないと言った
because she would not leave her father
彼女は父親から離れようとしなかったから
she was determined to go with him to the countryside
彼女は彼と一緒に田舎へ行くことを決心した
so that she could comfort and help him
彼女は彼を慰め助けるために
Poor Beauty was very grieved at first
最初はとても悲しかった
she was grieved by the loss of her fortune
彼女は財産を失ったことを悲しんだ
"but crying won't change my fortunes"
「でも泣いても運命は変わらない」
"I must try to make myself happy without wealth"
「富がなくても幸せになれるように努力しなければならない」
they came to their country house
彼らは田舎の家に来た
and the merchant and his three sons applied themselves to husbandry
商人とその3人の息子は農業に専念した
Beauty rose at four in the morning
朝の4時に美が目覚めた
and she hurried to clean the house
そして彼女は急いで家を掃除した

and she made sure dinner was ready
そして彼女は夕食の準備ができていることを確認した
in the beginning she found her new life very difficult
初めは彼女は新しい生活がとても困難だと感じた
because she had not been used to such work
彼女はそのような仕事に慣れていなかったので
but in less than two months she grew stronger
しかし、2ヶ月も経たないうちに彼女は強くなった
and she was healthier than ever before
そして彼女は以前よりも健康になった
after she had done her work she read
彼女は仕事を終えた後、本を読んだ
she played on the harpsichord
彼女はハープシコードを演奏した
or she sung whilst she spun silk
あるいは絹を紡ぎながら歌った
on the contrary, her two sisters did not know how to spend their time
それどころか、彼女の二人の姉妹は時間をどう過ごすべきかを知らなかった。
they got up at ten and did nothing but laze about all day
彼らは10時に起きて一日中何もせずに怠けていた
they lamented the loss of their fine clothes
彼らは上等な衣服を失ったことを嘆いた
and they complained about losing their acquaintances
そして彼らは知り合いを失ったことに不満を漏らした
"Have a look at our youngest sister," they said to each other
「私たちの末っ子の妹を見て」と彼らは互いに言った
"what a poor and stupid creature she is"
「彼女はなんて哀れで愚かな生き物なのだろう」
"it is mean to be content with so little"
「ほんの少しのもので満足するのは意地悪だ」
the kind merchant was of quite a different opinion
親切な商人は全く違う意見を持っていた
he knew very well that Beauty outshone her sisters

彼は彼女の美しさが姉妹たちを凌駕していることをよく知っていた

she outshone them in character as well as mind
彼女は性格的にも精神的にも彼らを凌駕していた

he admired her humility and her hard work
彼は彼女の謙虚さと勤勉さを賞賛した

but most of all he admired her patience
しかし何よりも彼は彼女の忍耐力に感心した

her sisters left her all the work to do
彼女の姉妹は彼女に全ての仕事を任せた

and they insulted her every moment
そして彼らは彼女を常に侮辱した

The family had lived like this for about a year
家族は1年ほどこのように暮らしていた

then the merchant got a letter from an accountant
すると商人は会計士から手紙を受け取った

he had an investment in a ship
彼は船に投資していた

and the ship had safely arrived
そして船は無事に到着した

this news turned the heads of the two eldest daughters
は二人の長女を驚かせた

they immediately had hopes of returning to town
彼らはすぐに町に戻ることを希望した

because they were quite weary of country life
彼らは田舎暮らしにかなり飽きていたので

they went to their father as he was leaving
彼らは父親が去ろうとしているところへ行った

they begged him to buy them new clothes
彼らは彼に新しい服を買ってくれるように頼んだ

dresses, ribbons, and all sorts of little things
ドレス、リボン、その他いろいろな小物

but Beauty asked for nothing
しかし美しさは何も求めなかった

because she thought the money wasn't going to be enough

お金が足りないと思ったから
there wouldn't be enough to buy everything her sisters wanted
姉妹が欲しがるもの全てを買うには十分ではないだろう

"What would you like, Beauty?" asked her father
「お嬢さん、何がほしい？」と父親は尋ねた。

"thank you, father, for the goodness to think of me," she said
「お父さん、私のことを思ってくれてありがとう」と彼女は言った

"father, be so kind as to bring me a rose"
「お父さん、どうか私にバラを持ってきてください」

"because no roses grow here in the garden"
「ここの庭にはバラが育たないから」

"and roses are a kind of rarity"
「そしてバラは一種の希少品です」

Beauty didn't really care for roses
美人はバラをあまり気にしていなかった

she only asked for something not to condemn her sisters
彼女はただ姉妹を非難しないよう求めただけだった

but her sisters thought she asked for roses for other reasons
しかし、彼女の姉妹は彼女がバラを求めた理由は他にもあると考えていた

"she did it just to look particular"
「彼女は特別に見えるためにそれをしただけ」

The kind man went on his journey
親切な男は旅に出た

but when he arrived they argued about the merchandise
しかし彼が到着すると彼らは商品について議論した

and after a lot of trouble he came back as poor as before
そして多くの苦労の末、彼は以前と同じように貧乏になって帰ってきた

he was within a couple of hours of his own house
彼は自分の家から数時間以内のところにいた

and he already imagined the joy of seeing his children
そして彼はすでに子供たちに会える喜びを想像していた

but when going through forest he got lost
しかし森を抜ける途中で道に迷ってしまった
it rained and snowed terribly
ひどい雨と雪が降った
the wind was so strong it threw him off his horse
風が強すぎて彼は馬から投げ出された
and night was coming quickly
そして夜が急速に近づいてきた
he began to think that he might starve
彼は飢え死にするかもしれないと考え始めた
and he thought that he might freeze to death
そして彼は凍死するかもしれないと思った
and he thought wolves may eat him
そして彼はオオカミに食べられてしまうかもしれないと思った
the wolves that he heard howling all round him
周囲で狼の遠吠えが聞こえた
but all of a sudden he saw a light
しかし突然、彼は光を見た
he saw the light at a distance through the trees
彼は木々の間から遠くの光を見た
when he got closer he saw the light was a palace
近づくと、その光は宮殿であることが分かった
the palace was illuminated from top to bottom
宮殿は上から下まで照らされていた
the merchant thanked God for his luck
商人は幸運を神に感謝した
and he hurried to the palace
そして彼は宮殿へ急いだ
but he was surprised to see no people in the palace
しかし、宮殿に人がいないことに驚いた。
the court yard was completely empty
中庭は完全に空っぽだった
and there was no sign of life anywhere
どこにも生命の兆候はなかった

his horse followed him into the palace
彼の馬は彼を追って宮殿に入った
and then his horse found large stable
そして彼の馬は大きな馬小屋を見つけた
the poor animal was almost famished
かわいそうな動物はほとんど飢えていました
so his horse went in to find hay and oats
そこで彼の馬は干し草とオート麦を探しに行きました
fortunately he found plenty to eat
幸運にも彼は食べるものをたくさん見つけた
and the merchant tied his horse up to the manger
そして商人は馬を飼い葉桶に繋ぎました
walking towards the house he saw no one
家に向かって歩いていると誰もいなかった
but in a large hall he found a good fire
しかし、大きなホールで彼は良い火を見つけた
and he found a table set for one
そして彼は一人用のテーブルを見つけた
he was wet from the rain and snow
彼は雨と雪で濡れていた
so he went near the fire to dry himself
そこで彼は体を乾かすために火のそばへ行った
"I hope the master of the house will excuse me"
「家の主人が私を許してくれることを願っています」
"I suppose it won't take long for someone to appear"
「誰かが現れるまで、そう時間はかからないだろう」
He waited a considerable time
彼はかなり長い間待った
he waited until it struck eleven, and still nobody came
彼は11時を待ったが、誰も来なかった
at last he was so hungry that he could wait no longer
ついに彼はあまりにも空腹になり、もう待てなくなった
。
he took some chicken and ate it in two mouthfuls
彼は鶏肉を少し取って二口で食べた

he was trembling while eating the food
彼は食べ物を食べながら震えていた
after this he drank a few glasses of wine
その後彼はワインを数杯飲んだ
growing more courageous he went out of the hall
彼は勇気を出してホールから出て行った
and he crossed through several grand halls
そして彼はいくつかの大きなホールを通り抜けた
he walked through the palace until he came into a chamber
彼は宮殿を歩き、ある部屋に入った。
a chamber which had an exceeding good bed in it
非常に良いベッドのある部屋
he was very much fatigued from his ordeal
彼は苦難のせいでとても疲れていた
and the time was already past midnight
そして時刻はすでに真夜中を過ぎていた
so he decided it was best to shut the door
そこで彼はドアを閉めるのが一番良いと判断した
and he concluded he should go to bed
そして彼は寝るべきだと結論した
It was ten in the morning when the merchant woke up
商人が目を覚ましたのは午前10時だった
just as he was going to rise he saw something
立ち上がろうとした瞬間、彼は何かを見た
he was astonished to see a clean set of clothes
彼はきれいな服を見て驚いた
in the place where he had left his dirty clothes
彼が汚れた服を置いた場所に
"certainly this palace belongs to some kind fairy"
「確かにこの宮殿はある種の妖精の所有物だ」
"a fairy who has seen and pitied me"
「私を見て哀れんだ妖精」
he looked through a window
彼は窓から外を見た
but instead of snow he saw the most delightful garden

しかし雪の代わりに彼はとても美しい庭園を見た
and in the garden were the most beautiful roses
庭には美しいバラが咲いていました
he then returned to the great hall
彼はその後大広間に戻った
the hall where he had had soup the night before
彼が前夜スープを食べたホール
and he found some chocolate on a little table
そして小さなテーブルの上にチョコレートを見つけた
"Thank you, good Madam Fairy," he said aloud
「ありがとう、優しい妖精さん」と彼は声を出して言った。
"thank you for being so caring"
「とても気遣ってくれてありがとう」
"I am extremely obliged to you for all your favours"
「あなたのご厚意に心から感謝いたします」
the kind man drank his chocolate
親切な男はチョコレートを飲んだ
and then he went to look for his horse
そして彼は馬を探しに行きました
but in the garden he remembered Beauty's request
しかし庭で彼は美女の願いを思い出した
and he cut off a branch of roses
そして彼はバラの枝を切り落とした
immediately he heard a great noise
すぐに大きな音が聞こえた
and he saw a terribly frightful Beast
そして彼は恐ろしく恐ろしい獣を見た
he was so scared that he was ready to faint
彼はとても怖かったので気を失いそうだった
"You are very ungrateful," said the Beast to him
「あなたは本当に恩知らずだ」と獣は彼に言った。
and the Beast spoke in a terrible voice
そして獣は恐ろしい声で言った
"I have saved your life by allowing you into my castle"

「私はあなたを城に入れることであなたの命を救った」
"and for this you steal my roses in return?"
「そしてそのお返しに私のバラを盗んだの？」
"The roses which I value beyond anything"
「私が何よりも大切にしているバラ」
"but you shall die for what you've done"
「しかし、あなたがしたことに対してあなたは死ぬことになるでしょう」
"I give you but a quarter of an hour to prepare yourself"
「準備に15分しか与えない」
"get yourself ready for death and say your prayers"
「死に備えて祈りを捧げなさい」
the merchant fell on his knees
商人はひざまずいた
and he lifted up both his hands
そして彼は両手を挙げた
"My lord, I beseech you to forgive me"
「主よ、どうか私をお許しください」
"I had no intention of offending you"
「あなたを怒らせるつもりはなかった」
"I gathered a rose for one of my daughters"
「娘のためにバラを摘みました」
"she asked me to bring her a rose"
「彼女は私にバラを持って来るように頼みました」
"I am not your lord, but I am a Beast," replied the monster
「私はあなたの主ではありませんが、私は獣です」と怪物は答えました
"I don't love compliments"
「私は褒め言葉が好きではない」
"I like people who speak as they think"
「私は自分の考えをそのまま話す人が好きです」
"do not imagine I can be moved by flattery"
「私がお世辞に心を動かされるとは思わないで」
"But you say you have got daughters"
「でも、あなたには娘がいるとおっしゃいますね」

"I will forgive you on one condition"
「一つの条件で許してあげるよ」
"one of your daughters must come to my palace willingly"
「あなたの娘の一人が私の宮殿に喜んで来なければなりません」
"and she must suffer for you"
「そして彼女はあなたのために苦しまなければならない」
"Let me have your word"
「あなたの言葉を聞いてください」
"and then you can go about your business"
「それから、自分の仕事に取り掛かってください」
"Promise me this:"
「私にこれを約束してください」
"if your daughter refuses to die for you, you must return within three months"
「もしあなたの娘があなたのために死ぬことを拒否するなら、あなたは3ヶ月以内に帰って来なければなりません」
the merchant had no intentions to sacrifice his daughters
商人は娘たちを犠牲にするつもりはなかった
but, since he was given time, he wanted to see his daughters once more
しかし、時間ができたので、もう一度娘たちに会いたかったのです
so he promised he would return
彼は戻ってくると約束した
and the Beast told him he might set out when he pleased
そして獣は彼に、いつでも出発していいと言った
and the Beast told him one more thing
そして獣はもう一つのことを彼に告げた
"you shall not depart empty handed"
「空手で出発してはならない」
"go back to the room where you lay"
「横になっていた部屋に戻りなさい」

"you will see a great empty treasure chest"
「大きな空の宝箱が見えるでしょう」
"fill the treasure chest with whatever you like best"
「宝箱に一番好きなものを詰め込んでください」
"and I will send the treasure chest to your home"
「そして宝箱をあなたの家に送ります」
and at the same time the Beast withdrew
そして同時に獣は退いた
"Well," said the good man to himself
「そうだな」と善良な男は独り言を言った
"if I must die, I shall at least leave something to my children"
「もし私が死ななければならないなら、少なくとも子供たちに何かを残すだろう」
so he returned to the bedchamber
そこで彼は寝室に戻った
and he found a great many pieces of gold
そして彼はたくさんの金貨を見つけた
he filled the treasure chest the Beast had mentioned
彼は獣が言っていた宝箱を満たした
and he took his horse out of the stable
そして彼は馬小屋から馬を連れ出した
the joy he felt when entering the palace was now equal to the grief he felt leaving it
宮殿に入るときに感じた喜びは、宮殿を出るときに感じた悲しみと同等だった。
the horse took one of the roads of the forest
馬は森の道の一つを進んだ
and in a few hours the good man was home
そして数時間後、その善良な男は家に帰った
his children came to him
彼の子供たちが彼のもとに来た
but instead of receiving their embraces with pleasure, he looked at them
しかし、彼は喜んで彼らの抱擁を受け入れる代わりに、

彼らを見つめた
he held up the branch he had in his hands
彼は手に持っていた枝を持ち上げました
and then he burst into tears
そして彼は泣き出した
"Beauty," he said, "please take these roses"
「美しい」と彼は言った。「このバラを受け取ってください」
"you can't know how costly these roses have been"
「このバラがどれだけ高価だったかは分からないだろう」
"these roses have cost your father his life"
「このバラのせいであなたのお父さんは命を落としたのです」
and then he told of his fatal adventure
そして彼は致命的な冒険について語った
immediately the two eldest sisters cried out
すぐに二人の姉が叫びました
and they said many mean things to their beautiful sister
そして彼らは美しい妹に多くの意地悪なことを言った
but Beauty did not cry at all
しかし美女は全く泣かなかった
"Look at the pride of that little wretch," said they
「あの小悪魔のプライドを見てみろ」と彼らは言った
"she did not ask for fine clothes"
「彼女は高級な服を求めなかった」
"she should have done what we did"
「彼女も私たちと同じことをすべきだった」
"she wanted to distinguish herself"
「彼女は自分を目立たせたかった」
"so now she will be the death of our father"
「それで今、彼女は私たちの父の死となるでしょう」
"and yet she does not shed a tear"
「それでも彼女は涙を流さない」
"Why should I cry?" answered Beauty

「なぜ泣かなければならないの？」と美女は答えた
"crying would be very needless"
「泣くことは全く無意味だ」
"my father will not suffer for me"
「父は私のために苦しむことはない」
"the monster will accept of one of his daughters"
「怪物は娘の一人を受け入れるだろう」
"I will offer myself up to all his fury"
「私は彼の怒りに身を捧げるつもりだ」
"I am very happy, because my death will save my father's life"
「私の死が父の命を救うことになるので、私はとても幸せです」
"my death will be a proof of my love"
「私の死は私の愛の証拠となるでしょう」
"No, sister," said her three brothers
「いいえ、姉さん」と彼女の3人の兄弟は言った。
"that shall not be"
「それはあってはならない」
"we will go find the monster"
「モンスターを探しに行こう」
"and either we will kill him..."
「そして我々は彼を殺すことになるだろう…」
"... or we will perish in the attempt"
「…さもなければ、我々はその試みで滅びるだろう」
"Do not imagine any such thing, my sons," said the merchant
「そんなことは想像しないでくれ、息子たちよ」と商人は言った。
"the Beast's power is so great that I have no hope you could overcome him"
「獣の力は強大なので、あなたがそれを打ち負かす望みはない」
"I am charmed with Beauty's kind and generous offer"
「私は美しさの優しく寛大な申し出に魅了されています」

"but I cannot accept to her generosity"
「しかし私は彼女の寛大さを受け入れることはできない」
"I am old, and I don't have long to live"
「私は年老いており、長く生きられない」
"so I can only loose a few years"
「だから、失うのは数年だけ」
"time which I regret for you, my dear children"
「私の愛しい子供たちよ、あなたたちにとって残念な時間」
"But father," said Beauty
「でもお父さん」美女は言った
"you shall not go to the palace without me"
「私なしで宮殿へ行ってはいけない」
"you cannot stop me from following you"
「私があなたを追いかけるのを止めることはできない」
nothing could convince Beauty otherwise
そうでなければ美を納得させることはできない
she insisted on going to the fine palace
彼女は立派な宮殿に行くことを主張した
and her sisters were delighted at her insistence
そして彼女の姉妹たちは彼女の主張に大喜びしました
The merchant was worried at the thought of losing his daughter
商人は娘を失うかもしれないと心配した
he was so worried that he had forgotten about the chest full of gold
彼は心配しすぎて、金が詰まった箱のことを忘れていた。
at night he retired to rest, and he shut his chamber door
夜、彼は休むために部屋のドアを閉めた。
then, to his great astonishment, he found the treasure by his bedside
そして驚いたことに、彼はベッドサイドに宝物を見つけた。

he was determined not to tell his children
彼は子供たちに言わないと決心した
if they knew, they would have wanted to return to town
もし知っていたら、彼らは町に戻りたかっただろう
and he was resolved not to leave the countryside
そして彼は田舎を離れないことを決意した
but he trusted Beauty with the secret
しかし彼は美しさに秘密を託した
she informed him that two gentlemen had came
彼女は二人の紳士が来たと彼に伝えた
and they made proposals to her sisters
そして彼らは彼女の姉妹にプロポーズをした
she begged her father to consent to their marriage
彼女は父親に結婚の同意を懇願した
and she asked him to give them some of his fortune
そして彼女は彼に財産の一部を寄付するよう頼んだ
she had already forgiven them
彼女はすでに彼らを許していた
the wicked creatures rubbed their eyes with onions
邪悪な生き物たちはタマネギで目をこすった
to force some tears when they parted with their sister
妹と別れるときに涙を流すために
but her brothers really were concerned
しかし彼女の兄弟たちは本当に心配していた
Beauty was the only one who did not shed any tears
美女だけが涙を流さなかった
she did not want to increase their uneasiness
彼女は彼らの不安を増大させたくなかった
the horse took the direct road to the palace
馬は宮殿への直行道を進んだ
and towards evening they saw the illuminated palace
そして夕方になると、彼らは明かりの灯った宮殿を見た
the horse took himself into the stable again
馬は再び馬小屋に戻った
and the good man and his daughter went into the great hall

そして善良な男と娘は大広間に入った
here they found a table splendidly served up
ここで彼らは豪華な料理が並べられたテーブルを見つけた
the merchant had no appetite to eat
商人は食べる気がなかった
but Beauty endeavoured to appear cheerful
しかし、美人は明るく見えるよう努めた
she sat down at the table and helped her father
彼女はテーブルに座り、父親を手伝った
but she also thought to herself:
しかし、彼女はまたこうも思いました。
"Beast surely wants to fatten me before he eats me"
「獣はきっと私を食べる前に太らせたいのだろう」
"that is why he provides such plentiful entertainment"
「だからこそ彼はこんなにも豊富なエンターテイメントを提供しているのです」
after they had eaten they heard a great noise
彼らが食事を終えると大きな音が聞こえた
and the merchant bid his unfortunate child farewell, with tears in his eyes
そして商人は目に涙を浮かべながら、不幸な子供に別れを告げた。
because he knew the Beast was coming
獣が来ることを知っていたから
Beauty was terrified at his horrid form
美女は彼の恐ろしい姿に恐怖した
but she took courage as well as she could
しかし彼女はできる限りの勇気を出した
and the monster asked her if she came willingly
そして怪物は彼女に、自ら来たのかと尋ねた
"yes, I have come willingly," she said trembling
「はい、喜んで来ました」と彼女は震えながら言った。
the Beast responded, "You are very good"
獣は答えた、「あなたはとても良い人だ」

"and I am greatly obliged to you; honest man"
「そして私はあなたにとても感謝しています。正直者よ」

"go your ways tomorrow morning"
「明日の朝、行きなさい」

"but never think of coming here again"
「しかし、二度とここに来ることは考えない」

"Farewell Beauty, farewell Beast," he answered
「さようなら美女、さようなら野獣」と彼は答えた

and immediately the monster withdrew
そしてすぐに怪物は退散した

"Oh, daughter," said the merchant
「ああ、娘さん」と商人は言った

and he embraced his daughter once more
そして彼はもう一度娘を抱きしめた

"I am almost frightened to death"
「死ぬほど怖いです」

"believe me, you had better go back"
「信じてください、戻った方がいいですよ」

"let me stay here, instead of you"
「あなたの代わりに、私がここにいさせてください」

"No, father," said Beauty, in a resolute tone
「いいえ、お父さん」と美女は毅然とした口調で言った。

"you shall set out tomorrow morning"
「明日の朝出発してください」

"leave me to the care and protection of providence"
「神の配慮と保護に私を任せてください」

nonetheless they went to bed
それでも彼らは寝た

they thought they would not close their eyes all night
彼らは一晩中目を閉じないだろうと思っていた

but just as they lay down they slept
しかし彼らは横になるとすぐに眠ってしまった

Beauty dreamed a fine lady came and said to her:

美女は、美しい女性がやって来てこう言う夢を見ました。

"I am content, Beauty, with your good will"
「美しい人よ、あなたの善意に私は満足しています」

"this good action of yours shall not go unrewarded"
「あなたのこの善行は報われないことはないだろう」

Beauty waked and told her father her dream
美女は目を覚まし、父親に夢を話した

the dream helped to comfort him a little
その夢は彼を少し慰めてくれた

but he could not help crying bitterly as he was leaving
しかし彼は去る時に激しく泣かずにはいられなかった

as soon as he was gone, Beauty sat down in the great hall and cried too
彼が去るとすぐに、美女も大広間に座り込み、泣きました

but she resolved not to be uneasy
しかし彼女は不安にならないように決心した

she decided to be strong for the little time she had left to live
彼女は残されたわずかな人生のために強くなろうと決心した

because she firmly believed the Beast would eat her
彼女は獣が自分を食べると固く信じていたので

however, she thought she might as well explore the palace
しかし、彼女は宮殿を探検してみるのもいいかもしれないと思った

and she wanted to view the fine castle
そして彼女は美しい城を見たいと思った

a castle which she could not help admiring
彼女が思わず感嘆した城

it was a delightfully pleasant palace
それはとても楽しい宮殿でした

and she was extremely surprised at seeing a door
彼女はドアを見てとても驚きました

and over the door was written that it was her room

ドアの上には彼女の部屋と書かれていた
she opened the door hastily
彼女は急いでドアを開けた
and she was quite dazzled with the magnificence of the room
彼女はその部屋の素晴らしさにすっかり魅了されてしまいました
what chiefly took up her attention was a large library
彼女の関心を最も惹きつけたのは大きな図書館だった
a harpsichord and several music books
ハープシコードと数冊の音楽本
"Well," said she to herself
「そうね」と彼女は自分に言った
"I see the Beast will not let my time hang heavy"
「獣は私の時間を重くしてはくれないだろう」
then she reflected to herself about her situation
そして彼女は自分の状況について考えた
"If I was meant to stay a day all this would not be here"
「もし私がここに1日滞在するつもりだったなら、これはすべてここにはなかったでしょう」
this consideration inspired her with fresh courage
この考えは彼女に新たな勇気を与えた
and she took a book from her new library
そして彼女は新しい図書館から本を取り出しました
and she read these words in golden letters:
そして彼女は金色の文字でこれらの言葉を読みました。
"Welcome Beauty, banish fear"
「美を歓迎し、恐怖を追い払おう」
"You are queen and mistress here"
「あなたはここでは女王であり女主人です」
"Speak your wishes, speak your will"
「あなたの願いを語りなさい、あなたの意志を語りなさい」
"Swift obedience meets your wishes here"
「ここでは素早い服従があなたの願いを満たします」

"Alas," said she, with a sigh
「ああ」と彼女はため息をつきながら言った。
"Most of all I wish to see my poor father"
「何よりも、私はかわいそうな父に会いたいのです」
"and I would like to know what he is doing"
「そして彼が何をしているのか知りたいのです」
As soon as she had said this she noticed the mirror
彼女がそう言うとすぐに鏡に気づいた
to her great amazement she saw her own home in the mirror
彼女は鏡に映った自分の家を見てとても驚いた。
her father arrived emotionally exhausted
彼女の父親は精神的に疲れ果てて到着した
her sisters went to meet him
彼女の姉妹は彼に会いに行った
despite their attempts to appear sorrowful, their joy was visible
彼らは悲しそうに見せようとしていたが、喜びは目に見えた。
a moment later everything disappeared
一瞬後、すべてが消えた
and Beauty's apprehensions disappeared too
そして美に対する不安も消えた
for she knew she could trust the Beast
彼女は獣を信頼できると知っていた
At noon she found dinner ready
正午に彼女は夕食の準備ができていることに気づいた
she sat herself down at the table
彼女はテーブルに座った
and she was entertained with a concert of music
そして彼女は音楽コンサートで楽しませられた
although she couldn't see anybody
彼女は誰にも会えなかったが
at night she sat down for supper again
夜、彼女は再び夕食に着席した
this time she heard the noise the Beast made

今度は獣が立てた音を聞いた
and she could not help being terrified
そして彼女は恐怖を感じずにはいられなかった
"Beauty," said the monster
「美しい」と怪物は言った
"do you allow me to eat with you?"
「一緒に食事をしてもいいですか？」
"do as you please," Beauty answered trembling
「好きなようにしてください」美女は震えながら答えた
"No," replied the Beast
「いいえ」獣は答えた
"you alone are mistress here"
「ここの女主人はあなただけです」
"you can send me away if I'm troublesome"
「面倒なら追い払ってもいいよ」
"send me away and I will immediately withdraw"
「私を追い払ってください。そうすればすぐに撤退します」
"But, tell me; do you not think I am very ugly?"
「でも、教えてください。あなたは私がとても醜いとは思いませんか？」
"That is true," said Beauty
「それは本当よ」と美女は言った
"I cannot tell a lie"
「嘘はつけない」
"but I believe you are very good natured"
「でも、あなたはとても優しい人だと思います」
"I am indeed," said the monster
「確かにそうだ」と怪物は言った
"But apart from my ugliness, I also have no sense"
「しかし、私の醜さは別として、私には分別がないのです」
"I know very well that I am a silly creature"
「私は自分が愚かな生き物だということをよく知っています」

"It is no sign of folly to think so," replied Beauty
「そう考えるのは愚かなことではありません」と美女は答えた。

"Eat then, Beauty," said the monster
「じゃあ食べなさいよ、美人さん」と怪物は言った

"try to amuse yourself in your palace"
「宮殿で楽しんでみてください」

"everything here is yours"
「ここにあるものはすべてあなたのものです」

"and I would be very uneasy if you were not happy"
「あなたが幸せでなかったら、私はとても不安になるでしょう」

"You are very obliging," answered Beauty
「とても親切ですね」と美女は答えた。

"I admit I am pleased with your kindness"
「あなたの優しさに嬉しく思います」

"and when I consider your kindness, I hardly notice your deformities"
「あなたの優しさを考えると、あなたの欠点はほとんど気になりません」

"Yes, yes," said the Beast, "my heart is good
「そうだ、そうだ」と獣は言った。「私の心は良い

"but although I am good, I am still a monster"
「しかし、私は善良ではあるが、それでも怪物だ」

"There are many men that deserve that name more than you"
「あなたよりもその名にふさわしい男はたくさんいる」

"and I prefer you just as you are"
「そして私は、ありのままのあなたが好きです」

"and I prefer you more than those who hide an ungrateful heart"
「そして私は恩知らずの心を隠す人々よりもあなたが好きです」

"if only I had some sense," replied the Beast
「もし私に分別があれば」と獣は答えた

"if I had sense I would make a fine compliment to thank

you"
「もし私に分別があれば、あなたに感謝するために素晴らしい賛辞を述べるでしょう」
"but I am so dull"
「でも私はとても退屈なの」
"I can only say I am greatly obliged to you"
「あなたには大変感謝しているとしか言えません」
Beauty ate a hearty supper
美女はボリュームたっぷりの夕食を食べた
and she had almost conquered her dread of the monster
そして彼女は怪物に対する恐怖をほぼ克服した
but she wanted to faint when the Beast asked her the next question
しかし、獣が次の質問をしたとき、彼女は気を失いそうになった
"Beauty, will you be my wife?"
「美人さん、私の妻になってくれませんか?」
she took some time before she could answer
彼女は答えるまでに少し時間がかかった
because she was afraid of making him angry
彼を怒らせるのが怖かったから
at last, however, she said "no, Beast"
しかし、ついに彼女は「ダメよ、獣」と言った。
immediately the poor monster hissed very frightfully
すぐにそのかわいそうな怪物は恐ろしい声をあげた
and the whole palace echoed
そして宮殿全体に響き渡った
but Beauty soon recovered from her fright
しかし美女はすぐに恐怖から立ち直った
because Beast spoke again in a mournful voice
獣は再び悲しげな声で話した。
"then farewell, Beauty"
「それではさようなら、美人さん」
and he only turned back now and then
そして彼は時々引き返すだけだった

to look at her as he went out
出かけるときに彼女を見るために
now Beauty was alone again
今、美は再び一人ぼっちになった
she felt a great deal of compassion
彼女は大きな同情を感じた
"Alas, it is a thousand pities"
「ああ、それは千の残念だ」
"anything so good natured should not be so ugly"
「こんなに善良なものは、こんなに醜いはずがない」
Beauty spent three months very contentedly in the palace
美女は宮殿で3ヶ月間をとても満足して過ごした
every evening the Beast paid her a visit
毎晩、獣は彼女を訪ねた
and they talked during supper
そして夕食中に彼らは話をした
they talked with common sense
彼らは常識を持って話した
but they didn't talk with what people call wittiness
しかし彼らは、いわゆる機知に富んだ話し方をしなかった
Beauty always discovered some valuable character in the Beast
美は常に獣の中に価値ある特徴を発見した
and she had gotten used to his deformity
そして彼女は彼の奇形に慣れていた
she didn't dread the time of his visit anymore
彼女はもう彼の訪問を恐れていなかった
now she often looked at her watch
彼女は今ではよく時計を見るようになった
and she couldn't wait for it to be nine o'clock
そして彼女は9時になるのを待ちきれなかった
because the Beast never missed coming at that hour
獣は必ずその時間にやって来るから
there was only one thing that concerned Beauty

美しさに関することはただ一つだけだった
every night before she went to bed the Beast asked her the same question
毎晩寝る前に獣は同じ質問をした
the monster asked her if she would be his wife
怪物は彼女に妻になってくれるかと尋ねた
one day she said to him, "Beast, you make me very uneasy"
ある日彼女は彼に言いました。「獣よ、あなたは私をとても不安にさせるわ」
"I wish I could consent to marry you"
「あなたと結婚することに同意できればいいのですが」
"but I am too sincere to make you believe I would marry you"
「でも、私はあなたと結婚するなんて信じさせるほど誠実ではない」
"our marriage will never happen"
「私たちの結婚は決して実現しないだろう」
"I shall always see you as a friend"
「私はいつもあなたを友達として見ています」
"please try to be satisfied with this"
「これで満足してみてください」
"I must be satisfied with this," said the Beast
「これで満足しなくちゃ」と獣は言った
"I know my own misfortune"
「私は自分の不幸を知っている」
"but I love you with the tenderest affection"
「でも私はあなたを心から愛しています」
"However, I ought to consider myself as happy"
「しかし、私は自分自身を幸せだと考えるべきだ」
"and I should be happy that you will stay here"
「そしてあなたがここにいてくれることを私は嬉しく思います」
"promise me never to leave me"
「私を決して見捨てないと約束してください」
Beauty blushed at these words

美女はこの言葉を聞いて顔を赤らめた
one day Beauty was looking in her mirror
ある日、美女は鏡を見ていた
her father had worried himself sick for her
彼女の父親は彼女のことを心配していた
she longed to see him again more than ever
彼女は今まで以上に彼にもう一度会いたいと願っていた
"I could promise never to leave you entirely"
「あなたを完全に見捨てることはないと約束できます」
"but I have so great a desire to see my father"
「でも、私は父に会いたいと強く願っているんです」
"I would be impossibly upset if you say no"
「もしあなたがノーと言ったら、私はとんでもなく怒るでしょう」
"I had rather die myself," said the monster
「私は死んだほうがましだ」と怪物は言った
"I would rather die than make you feel uneasiness"
「不安を感じさせるくらいなら死んだほうがましだ」
"I will send you to your father"
「私はあなたをあなたの父のところへ送ります」
"you shall remain with him"
「あなたは彼と一緒にいなさい」
"and this unfortunate Beast will die with grief instead"
「そしてこの不幸な獣は悲しみのうちに死ぬだろう」
"No," said Beauty, weeping
「いいえ」美女は泣きながら言った
"I love you too much to be the cause of your death"
「私はあなたを愛しすぎていて、あなたの死の原因にはなり得ない」
"I give you my promise to return in a week"
「一週間以内に戻ってくると約束します」
"You have shown me that my sisters are married"
「あなたは私の姉妹が結婚していることを教えてくれました」
"and my brothers have gone to the army"

「そして私の兄弟は軍隊に行きました」
"let me stay a week with my father, as he is alone"
「父は独り身なので、一週間父のところに泊まらせてください」
"You shall be there tomorrow morning," said the Beast
「明日の朝にはそこにいるだろう」と獣は言った
"but remember your promise"
「でも約束を忘れないで」
"You need only lay your ring on a table before you go to bed"
「寝る前に指輪をテーブルの上に置くだけでいい」
"and then you will be brought back before the morning"
「そして朝までには連れ戻されるでしょう」
"Farewell dear Beauty," sighed the Beast
「さようなら、愛しい人よ」と獣はため息をついた。
Beauty went to bed very sad that night
美女はその夜とても悲しそうに眠りについた
because she didn't want to see Beast so worried
獣が心配しているのを見たくなかったから
the next morning she found herself at her father's home
翌朝、彼女は父親の家にいることに気づいた
she rung a little bell by her bedside
彼女はベッドサイドの小さなベルを鳴らした
and the maid gave a loud shriek
メイドは大きな悲鳴をあげた
and her father ran upstairs
そして彼女の父親は階段を駆け上がった
he thought he was going to die with joy
彼は喜びのうちに死ぬだろうと思った
he held her in his arms for quarter of an hour
彼は15分間彼女を抱きしめた
eventually the first greetings were over
結局最初の挨拶は終わった
Beauty began to think of getting out of bed
美女はベッドから起き上がることを考え始めた

but she realized she had brought no clothes
しかし彼女は服を持ってこなかったことに気づいた
but the maid told her she had found a box
しかしメイドは箱を見つけたと彼女に言った
the large trunk was full of gowns and dresses
大きなトランクはガウンやドレスでいっぱいだった
each gown was covered with gold and diamonds
それぞれのドレスは金とダイヤモンドで覆われていた
Beauty thanked Beast for his kind care
美女は野獣の優しい気遣いに感謝した。
and she took one of the plainest of the dresses
そして彼女は最もシンプルなドレスの一つを選んだ
she intended to give the other dresses to her sisters
彼女は他のドレスを姉妹にあげるつもりだった
but at that thought the chest of clothes disappeared
しかしその考えに、衣服の入った箱は消えた
Beast had insisted the clothes were for her only
獣は服は自分だけのものだと主張した
her father told her that this was the case
彼女の父親は彼女にこう言った
and immediately the trunk of clothes came back again
するとすぐに衣服の入ったトランクが戻ってきました
Beauty dressed herself with her new clothes
美女は新しい服を着た
and in the meantime maids went to find her sisters
そしてその間にメイドたちは彼女の姉妹を探しに行った
both her sister were with their husbands
彼女の姉妹は二人とも夫と一緒にいた
but both her sisters were very unhappy
しかし、彼女の姉妹は二人ともとても不幸でした
her eldest sister had married a very handsome gentleman
彼女の姉はとてもハンサムな紳士と結婚した
but he was so fond of himself that he neglected his wife
しかし彼は自分自身を愛しすぎて妻を無視した
her second sister had married a witty man

彼女の二番目の姉は気の利いた男と結婚した
but he used his wittiness to torment people
しかし彼はその機知を人々を苦しめるために使った
and he tormented his wife most of all
そして彼は妻を最も苦しめた
Beauty's sisters saw her dressed like a princess
美女の姉妹は彼女が王女のような服を着ているのを見た
and they were sickened with envy
そして彼らは嫉妬に苛まれていた
now she was more beautiful than ever
彼女は今、かつてないほど美しくなった
her affectionate behaviour could not stifle their jealousy
彼女の愛情深い態度は彼らの嫉妬を抑えることができなかった
she told them how happy she was with the Beast
彼女は獣と一緒にいるのがどんなに幸せか彼らに話した
and their jealousy was ready to burst
そして彼らの嫉妬は爆発寸前だった
They went down into the garden to cry about their misfortune
彼らは庭に降りて、自分たちの不幸を嘆きました
"In what way is this little creature better than us?"
「この小さな生き物は、どんな点で私たちより優れているのでしょうか？」
"Why should she be so much happier?"
「なぜ彼女はそんなに幸せになるべきなの？」
"Sister," said the older sister
「姉さん」と姉は言った
"a thought just struck my mind"
「ある考えが頭に浮かんだ」
"let us try to keep her here for more than a week"
「彼女を1週間以上ここに留めておくように努力しましょう」
"perhaps this will enrage the silly monster"
「おそらくこれは愚かな怪物を激怒させるだろう」

"because she would have broken her word"
「彼女は約束を破っただろうから」
"and then he might devour her"
「そして彼は彼女を食い尽くすかもしれない」
"that's a great idea," answered the other sister
「それは素晴らしい考えよ」ともう一人の姉妹は答えた。
"we must show her as much kindness as possible"
「私たちは彼女にできる限りの優しさを示さなければなりません」
the sisters made this their resolution
姉妹はこれを決意した
and they behaved very affectionately to their sister
そして彼らは妹に対してとても愛情深く振る舞った
poor Beauty wept for joy from all their kindness
貧しい美女は彼らの優しさに喜びの涙を流した
when the week was expired, they cried and tore their hair
1週間が過ぎると、彼らは泣きながら髪の毛をむしり取った。
they seemed so sorry to part with her
彼らは彼女と別れるのがとても残念に思えた
and Beauty promised to stay a week longer
そして美しさは1週間長く続くと約束した
In the meantime, Beauty could not help reflecting on herself
その間、美は自分自身を反省せずにはいられなかった
she worried what she was doing to poor Beast
彼女はかわいそうな獣に何をしているのか心配した
she know that she sincerely loved him
彼女は心から彼を愛していたことを知っている
and she really longed to see him again
そして彼女は本当に彼にもう一度会いたかった
the tenth night she spent at her father's too
10日目の夜も彼女は父親の家で過ごした
she dreamed she was in the palace garden
彼女は宮殿の庭にいる夢を見た

and she dreamt she saw the Beast extended on the grass
そして彼女は夢の中で獣が草の上に伸びているのを見た
he seemed to reproach her in a dying voice
彼は死にそうな声で彼女を非難しているようだった
and he accused her of ingratitude
そして彼は彼女の恩知らずを非難した
Beauty woke up from her sleep
美女は眠りから目覚めた
and she burst into tears
そして彼女は泣き出した
"Am I not very wicked?"
「私はそんなに邪悪な人間ではないでしょうか？」
"Was it not cruel of me to act so unkindly to the Beast?"
「私が獣に対してこんなにも無慈悲な行為をしたのは残酷ではなかったでしょうか？」
"Beast did everything to please me"
「獣は私を喜ばせるためにあらゆることをした」
"Is it his fault that he is so ugly?"
「彼がこんなに醜いのは彼のせいですか？」
"Is it his fault that he has so little wit?"
「彼がそんなに知恵がないのは彼のせいですか？」
"He is kind and good, and that is sufficient"
「彼は優しくて良い人です。それで十分です」
"Why did I refuse to marry him?"
「なぜ私は彼との結婚を拒否したのか？」
"I should be happy with the monster"
「モンスターに満足するべきだ」
"look at the husbands of my sisters"
「私の姉妹の夫たちを見てください」
"neither wittiness, nor a being handsome makes them good"
「機知に富んでいるとか、ハンサムであるとかいうことは、彼らを善良にするわけではない」
"neither of their husbands makes them happy"
「どちらの夫も彼女たちを幸せにしてくれない」
"but virtue, sweetness of temper, and patience"

「しかし、美徳、優しい気質、そして忍耐」
"these things make a woman happy"
「これらは女性を幸せにする」
"and the Beast has all these valuable qualities"
「そしてその獣はこれらすべての価値ある性質を持っている」
"it is true; I do not feel the tenderness of affection for him"
「それは本当です。私は彼に対して愛情の優しさを感じません」
"but I find I have the highest gratitude for him"
「しかし、私は彼に最大の感謝の気持ちを抱いています」
"and I have the highest esteem of him"
「そして私は彼を最も尊敬しています」
"and he is my best friend"
「そして彼は私の親友です」
"I will not make him miserable"
「彼を不幸にはさせない」
"If were I to be so ungrateful I would never forgive myself"
「もし私がそんなに恩知らずだったら、私は自分自身を決して許さないだろう」
Beauty put her ring on the table
美女は指輪をテーブルの上に置いた
and she went to bed again
そして彼女はまたベッドに横になった
scarce was she in bed before she fell asleep
彼女はベッドに入るとすぐに眠りに落ちた
she woke up again the next morning
彼女は翌朝また目覚めた
and she was overjoyed to find herself in the Beast's palace
そして彼女は自分が野獣の宮殿にいることに大喜びしました
she put on one of her nicest dress to please him
彼女は彼を喜ばせるために最も素敵なドレスを着た
and she patiently waited for evening

そして彼女は辛抱強く夕方を待った
at last the wished-for hour came
ついに待ち望んだ時が来た
the clock struck nine, yet no Beast appeared
時計は9時を打ったが、獣は現れなかった
Beauty then feared she had been the cause of his death
美女は自分が彼の死の原因ではないかと恐れた
she ran crying all around the palace
彼女は泣きながら宮殿中を走り回った
after having sought for him everywhere, she remembered her dream
彼をあちこち探し回った後、彼女は夢を思い出した
and she ran to the canal in the garden
そして彼女は庭の運河まで走って行きました
there she found poor Beast stretched out
そこで彼女は哀れな獣が横たわっているのを見つけた
and she was sure she had killed him
そして彼女は彼を殺したと確信した
she threw herself upon him without any dread
彼女は何の恐れもなく彼に飛びかかった
his heart was still beating
彼の心臓はまだ動いていた
she fetched some water from the canal
彼女は運河から水を汲んだ
and she poured the water on his head
そして彼女は彼の頭に水を注ぎました
the Beast opened his eyes and spoke to Beauty
野獣は目を開けて美女に話しかけた
"You forgot your promise"
「約束を忘れた」
"I was so heartbroken to have lost you"
「あなたを失ったことはとても悲しかった」
"I resolved to starve myself"
「私は飢え死にしようと決心した」
"but I have the happiness of seeing you once more"

「でも、もう一度あなたに会えて幸せです」
"so I have the pleasure of dying satisfied"
「だから私は満足して死ぬ喜びを得る」
"No, dear Beast," said Beauty, "you must not die"
「いいえ、愛しい獣よ」美女は言った。「あなたは死んではいけないわ」
"Live to be my husband"
「私の夫になるために生きてください」
"from this moment I give you my hand"
「この瞬間から私はあなたに手を差し伸べます」
"and I swear to be none but yours"
「そして私はあなたのものになることを誓います」
"Alas! I thought I had only a friendship for you"
「ああ！私はあなたとただの友情でいたいと思っていた」
"but the grief I now feel convinces me;"
「しかし、今私が感じている悲しみが私を納得させます。」
"I cannot live without you"
「あなたなしでは生きていけない」
Beauty scarce had said these words when she saw a light
美女が光を見たとき、彼女はこれらの言葉を言った
the palace sparkled with light
宮殿は光で輝いていた
fireworks lit up the sky
花火が空を照らした
and the air filled with music
空気は音楽で満たされた
everything gave notice of some great event
すべてが大きな出来事を予告していた
but nothing could hold her attention
しかし、彼女の注意を引くものは何もなかった
she turned to her dear Beast
彼女は愛する獣に目を向けた
the Beast for whom she trembled with fear

彼女が恐怖に震えた獣
but her surprise was great at what she saw!
しかし、彼女は見たものにとても驚きました！
the Beast had disappeared
獣は姿を消した
instead she saw the loveliest prince
代わりに彼女は最も美しい王子様を見た
she had put an end to the spell
彼女は呪いを解いた
a spell under which he resembled a Beast
彼を獣のような姿にした呪文
this prince was worthy of all her attention
この王子は彼女の注目に値する人物だった
but she could not help but ask where the Beast was
しかし彼女は獣がどこにいるのか尋ねずにはいられなかった
"You see him at your feet," said the prince
「あなたの足元に彼がいるのが見えますよ」と王子は言った
"A wicked fairy had condemned me"
「邪悪な妖精が私を非難した」
"I was to remain in that shape until a beautiful princess agreed to marry me"
「美しい王女が私と結婚するまで、私はその姿のままでいなければならなかった」
"the fairy hid my understanding"
「妖精は私の理解を隠した」
"you were the only one generous enough to be charmed by the goodness of my temper"
「私の気質の良さに魅了されるほど寛大な人はあなただけだった」
Beauty was happily surprised
美人は嬉しい驚きを感じた
and she gave the charming prince her hand
そして彼女は魅力的な王子に手を差し出した

they went together into the castle
彼らは一緒に城に入った
and Beauty was overjoyed to find her father in the castle
美女は城で父親を見つけて大喜びしました
and her whole family were there too
彼女の家族全員もそこにいた
even the beautiful lady that appeared in her dream was there
夢に現れた美しい女性もそこにいた
"Beauty," said the lady from the dream
「美しい」と夢の中の女性は言った
"come and receive your reward"
「来て報酬を受け取ってください」
"you have preferred virtue over wit or looks"
「あなたは知恵や容姿よりも美徳を優先した」
"and you deserve someone in whom these qualities are united"
「そしてあなたは、これらの資質を兼ね備えた人に値するのです」
"you are going to be a great queen"
「あなたは偉大な女王になるでしょう」
"I hope the throne will not lessen your virtue"
「王位があなたの徳を損なわないことを願います」
then the fairy turned to the two sisters
それから妖精は二人の姉妹のほうを向いた
"I have seen inside your hearts"
「私はあなたたちの心の中を見ました」
"and I know all the malice your hearts contain"
「そして私はあなたの心にある悪意をすべて知っています」
"you two will become statues"
「あなたたち二人は彫像になるだろう」
"but you will keep your minds"
「しかし、あなたは心を留めるでしょう」
"you shall stand at the gates of your sister's palace"
「あなたは妹の宮殿の門に立つでしょう」

"your sister's happiness shall be your punishment"
「妹の幸せがあなたの罰となる」

"you won't be able to return to your former states"
「以前の状態には戻れないだろう」

"unless, you both admit your faults"
「ただし、二人とも自分の過ちを認めない限りは」

"but I am foresee that you will always remain statues"
「しかし、私はあなたがいつまでも彫像のままであると予見しています」

"pride, anger, gluttony, and idleness are sometimes conquered"
「プライド、怒り、貪欲、怠惰は、時には克服される」

"but the conversion of envious and malicious minds are miracles"
「しかし、嫉妬と悪意に満ちた心の改心は奇跡である」

immediately the fairy gave a stroke with her wand
すぐに妖精は杖で一撃を与えた

and in a moment all that were in the hall were transported
そして一瞬のうちにホールにいた全員が

they had gone into the prince's dominions
彼らは王子の領土に入っていた

the prince's subjects received him with joy
王子の臣下たちは喜んで彼を迎えた

the priest married Beauty and the Beast
司祭は美女と野獣と結婚した

and he lived with her many years
そして彼は彼女と何年も一緒に暮らした

and their happiness was complete
そして彼らの幸福は完璧だった

because their happiness was founded on virtue
彼らの幸福は徳に基づいていたから

**The End**
終わり

**www.tranzlaty.com**

www.ingramcontent.com/pod-product-compliance
Lightning Source LLC
Chambersburg PA
CBHW012011090526
44590CB00026B/3969